Thank you to all those who have supported me and been a part of the journey that has led me here. Including the friends who have served alongside me in the creation of this book:

Cover design: McCall Cox
Author Photo: Josh Cummins
Editors: Angela Brickle, Jess Embree, Tiffany Cates, Bria Gilmore, Shannon Wolf, Sarah Schott and Cindy Hungerford
Marketing Team: Ty Williams, Joey Hungerford, Josiah Richwine, Sennua Lawson, Sarah Schott and Sandy Johnson

SetApartOne
ISBN-13: 978-0692150566
ISBN-10: 0692150560
BISAC: Religion / General

MASKED BY A MYRIAD OF CIRCUMSTANCES

HOLLY HUNGERFORD

Dedication: to my dad, who showed me God's love and faithfulness in so many ways throughout my life. I know His love because of your real life example. I love you!

Table of Contents

TO THE
FAITHFUL
YOU SHOW
YOURSELF
FAITHFUL,
TO THE
BLAMELESS
YOU SHOW
YOURSELF
BLAMELESS.

PSALM 18:25

Preface

Our generation is one of the most incredible generations to ever walk the Earth. We create, we empower, we fly, we literally have information at our fingertips. We were made to set a divine purpose in motion. Yet, our incredibly great calling is matched by equally great opposition.

You see, the enemy is unable to tell the future, to know God's plans, or our hearts desires, but this being was created with an angelic nature, therefore he can feel and sense the shift in the atmosphere. And he's afraid. As he should be. So with our greatness comes great tribulation and trial. He has always tried to win his battles against believers in the area of our minds, so he returns to this area once more hoping to defeat us and ultimately the Father.

As a generation created to lead and awaken, he seeks to silence our voices through inner struggle. This is the story of the bold and brave children of our generation, seeking to serve, and being met with struggle. Here we meet. But in the midst of tragedy, we have been given triumph.

"Yea, though I walk through the valley of the shadow of death, I will fear no evil: for thou art with me; thy rod and thy staff they comfort me."
Psalm 23:4

We must embrace this struggle for ultimately it will lead us to our purpose as a generation. Unlike any before us, we will be a part of seeking and saving the lost, in incredibly new ways and at the end of our days we will hear- *"well done my good and faithful servant"* (Matthew 25:23).

We win.

This book came out of a dream I didn't know I had, through a journey with Jesus I didn't know I had signed up for. My hope is that through my own vulnerability, through my journal entries and personal stories, you will see that you are not alone in this struggle and that Christ has healing in mind for you.

This book is meant to be a place for you to examine, grow, and gain tools needed to live victoriously. Write in the columns, invite a friend to join you, and create within these pages. Add color and highlights to areas you need to revisit. This is your book. Take charge dear friend! I hope to meet you soon!

Holly Hungerford

Introduction

For we do not have a high priest who is unable to empathize with our weaknesses, but we have one who has been tempted in every way, just as we are—yet he did not sin. Let us then approach God's throne of grace with confidence, so that we may receive mercy and find grace to help us in our time of need.

Hebrew 4:15-16

Insecurity has become an epidemic sweeping our generation in varied forms and fashions, but nonetheless paralyzing us on our journey toward the future God has for us.

Insecurity comes and disengages our hearts and wares against our minds. Were I to say defeating it was an easy task, I would nonetheless be wrong. A painful task at best to war against, yet vital to our survival and very being.

According to the ADAA (Anxiety and Depression Association of America) 40 million adults, 18 and up, struggle with anxiety. That's 18% of the US population. Many disorders are twice as likely to take place in women than men. The ADAA says anxiety disorders are the most common mental illness in the United States.[1] Anxiety seems to be a tool the enemy is using to silence and destroy this generation; a ploy to take our voice and our vibrant spirits and turn them to dust. For the purpose of unity in this book I have used the word "anxiety" because that has been the tool the enemy has used on me and many around me, but should yours be depression, fear, or another insecurity based pain, feel free to replace anxiety with your own personal struggle.

This book is not another book about stats and self-help, this book is about starting a journey to deeper healing with your Creator, one that will forever leave you changed and challenged to see others experience this same freedom. I have

---

[1] N. *Facts and Statistics.* Accessed May 2015 through https://adaa.org/about-adaa/press-room/facts-statistics#

walked this road myself, and want to lead you and see you taste sweet freedom from the Father. It won't be easy. There will be days when you want to give up and forsake all truth for temporary comfort, but don't, my friend, it will be so worth it in the long haul. Pursue wholeness. Then and only then, will you taste a peace never known before.

My story

I grew up as a child steeped in fear. You could almost say the enemy of my soul had a plan to destroy me from day one. As a child I would often have excruciating nightmares and wake up terrified and quickly retreat to my parents' floor or bed. I can remember even being 21 and having such a horrific nightmare that I snuck into their room and slept on the floor- close to the door- terrified but equally embarrassed.

My childhood was one for the books! Full of backyard activities, living room tent creations, shenanigans, and family trips. But like any family, we had our own version of dysfunction and with love I also experienced fear and insecurity intertwined. Finding myself broken and longing for acceptance at the age of 18 I entered into a destructive relationship (caving to peer pressure), that led to the loss of my identity and wellbeing, and ultimately my trust in God and others. Through that unbroken seal, anxiety entered. Panic attacks came and fear surged. Not only did I hate what happened to me, but I hated who I was and what I had become, and the enemy used every opportunity to remind me of my foul conduct.

When I finally decided to start dating again, I would feel out of control, this was especially true when similarities were present within the relationship. It was there that my uninvited friend would return, reminding me that I was a failure and could no longer handle the life I had been given. I would shrink into these horribly dark places with my thoughts as my only friends. The uncontrollable swirls of emotions and uncertainty would almost deny my next breath, and then I realized what a master manipulator of pain. How could I not see the fingerprint of my very enemy devising my destruction? As I began to continue living but limping with these same pains, I would encounter others with similar stories: similar pain and equal opposition. And so began a journey that has led me here. On a road to healing, and hoping to take the hands of others and lead them there. On a road with Jesus, the Divine Healer.

No one loves to air their dirty laundry or aspires to write a book about their dark secrets, but what we hide cannot heal, and therein lies the plan of our enemy. This journey has been dark at times and absolutely spectacular in others, but each twist and turn has led me to a sweet freedom that can only be tasted by a deep healing found within my Savior. He was there for me and He'll be there for you. Let's walk this out dear friend, and see how He will do it!

Exposing the Lies

*"But if we walk in the light, as he is in the light, we have
fellowship with one another, and the blood of Jesus, his
Son, purifies us from all sin." 1 John 1:7*

Steps of faith.

I can remember it like it was yesterday. I
sat in church on a Wednesday night and at the end
of service my pastor said he could sense there was
someone who had been deeply struggling with fear.
Everyone bowed their heads and he asked that the
individual raise their hand, in faith and surrender
to God. I had done this so many times but wanted
to be obedient and honest. I did, and in that
moment a physical manifestation of fear lifted off
of me. I can't describe it but I'll try. It was like a

giant weight had been lifted off my shoulders. All of a sudden I sensed a deeper peace within me and a boldness I had not yet known while carrying this deep fear. I was free.

That following weekend my family was out of town, an event that would normally cause me to have a friend over, but I decided to stay home alone, something I had never done, and use my new found freedom.

This is where we begin our journey. As lost children looking for a path home, we must recognize that we are not those who sit in darkness, but children of the light (Ephesians 5:8). To experience light in our lives we must turn to the Word of God and get it deep in our spirit. We have to take the words of Christ and live them out daily by choosing to regularly meditate on His truth so that we are able to discern the lies. Especially since the counterfeits are often so deeply intertwined with fragmented truth.

Jesus said that if we seek Him with all our heart, mind, soul and strength- we WILL be found by Him. Obedience. The call is for us to seek Him, and if we obey His heart's call, He promises to meet us! When we meet Him and develop intimacy with Him, we experience the true blessing of being His children. As Pastor Reggie Scarborough said, "when we seek the Healer, the Provider, the Prince of Peace, when we seek Him, we receive the blessings of being in fellowship with Him: healing, provision, peace…but seek the Healer, not the healing." In other words, the blessings are a byproduct once you have the right focus. They follow the Good Father who desires to give us good gifts. But what child can expect gifts from a father they are not in relationship with?

A real relationship with Daddy, our Father God, is what life is all about. A byproduct of being in relationship with Him is experiencing the blessing and security of really knowing Him, and in turn knowing ourselves. Matthew 10:39 in the Message translation says *"If you don't go all the way with me, through thick and thin, you don't deserve me. If your first concern is to look after yourself, you'll never find yourself.* ***But if you forget about yourself and look to me, you'll find both yourself and me"*** (emphasis mine).

The enemy of our souls knows that if we know the truth (I mean really know it) about who we are and whose we are, we will be a force that hell cannot reckon with. Our spiritual authority and understanding is a major ingredient in our healing. We have to recognize the power we've been given and put it into practice.

Each one of us knows the pain of confronting lies, but it is absolutely necessary to our wholeness. I was on the phone this week with a friend, and then met another for coffee, and both conversations were about confronting the lies and being able to make godly decisions for their futures based on the truth. I am so angry with the enemy because he has lied to countless people, creating a belief that settling for less than God's best is okay, and even normal. Not so. God did not send His son to die for you to have a semi-fulfilling, semi-joyful, semi-enjoyable life. Not so my friend. He wants the best for you! Don't believe the lies anymore, start to expose them!

We have to be conscious of the enemy's deception and choose to boldly walk in truth. Galatians 5:7-10 says *"You were running a good race. Who cut in on you to keep you from obeying the truth? That kind of persuasion does not come from the one who calls you. "A little yeast works through the whole batch of dough." I am confident in the Lord that you will take no other view. The one who is throwing you into confusion, whoever that may be, will have to pay the penalty."* Let's not let a little bit of yeast, a little bit of deception, destroy the entire destiny of our lives.

Let's expose the darkness to the marvelous light of Christ! Let's look at our pain and expose the enemy's purpose in it. His plan is to put you in situations and relationships that cause you to question the faithfulness and trustworthiness of

God. Often we can't quickly get to the root of what is actually going on because it's a jumbled up mess. In those moments, thought provoking questions are key. Below are some questions that will help you get to the root of what is going on in your mind, body, spirit and heart, as you walk through a situation. Let's try it! Take out a journal or a blank piece of paper and let's answer the questions below.

An exercise on exposing the lies:
What does this thought create in me?:

*Does this thought create peace or confusion?
*Does this thought push me closer to God or further from Him?
*Does this thought excite me for the future or cause me to withdraw from others in the present?
*Am I experiencing clarity or chaos when I dwell on this thought?

Example: _"I feel like I'm wasting my life, I'm 26 and ready to do what God has called me to do. Why am I not being used, why am I still here, what am I supposed to do?"_
Feelings: stomach in knots, worry, disconnect from God, anxiety.

The diagram below shows you what happens as those negative thoughts come into your mind. The thought creates an insecurity and that insecurity takes root in a destructive area in your life. Maybe through fear, discontentment, shame or self-loathing. Our responsibility is to identify that root and bring it to Jesus.

Take a few minutes and expose. Shine a light on the places of darkness (hidden), that are creating pain in your life. Use the questions from Page 25 to begin this process.

Diagram of Insecurity

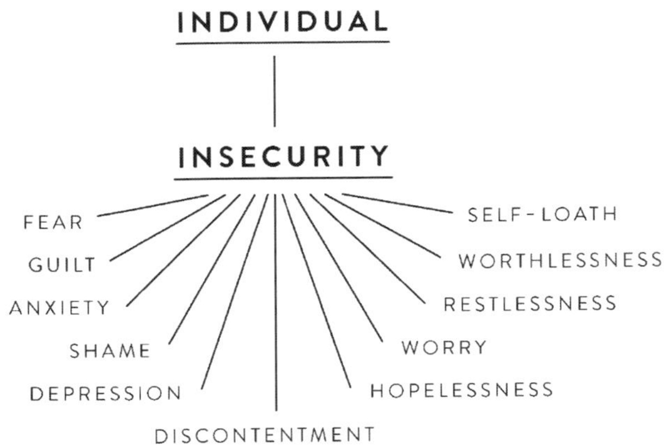

We have to train our hearts to be anxious for nothing (Philippians 4:6-7). As we know from scripture, God is NOT the author of confusion (1 Corinthians 14:33), but He gives us peace. Therefore when anxiety hits, we can be certain that our Savior has the remedy, since He did not create it. That is our God-given right and gift: peace. The enemy of our souls knows that if he can get us in a "tizzy" of confusion, we are off to a good start on the road to self-destruction. Our minds will begin to center on that one thought: "I'll never get married," "I'll never have a career," "I'm always going to fail," and off we go. All he has to do is plant a seed and we do the rest with our focus.

How easily we are lead astray when we don't know who we are in Christ.

So let's take the prescription. Lets begin to really discover who we are and whose we are. If we could deeply and completely settle this truth, we would live lives that exemplify the grace, power and love of the King, and we would be confident and unashamed in our pursuit of life. We wouldn't allow fears, others' words, or painful experiences to hold us down because we would understand that we are being held by a GREATER power. Living out of that power gives us the opportunity to expose the enemy's lies and live lives that are bold and authentic.

God wants His kids to live boldly and confidently, experiencing peace and enjoying His absolute favor and love for us. Unhindered by the worries of this life, but focused on the prize. Jesus talks about this person in Matthew 13:23, their heart is the heart and life that exemplifies good soil, *"someone who hears the Word and understands it. This is the one who produces a crop, yielding a hundred, sixty or thirty times what was sown."* I picture that life as someone who really stops, absorbs God's Word, allows it to change them, and then lives vibrantly because they've been changed. That person draws others into the heart of God through their freedom that invites.

I don't know about you, but when I'm with someone I love or even texting that person, my persona changes. I smile. I laugh. I cry. I linger in their presence. That's what it feels like when we begin to really understand who God is and the degree to which He loves us. We smile. We laugh. We cry. We linger in His presence, and because of those experiences we live changed!

You can always tell, in passing, those who have an incredible and real relationship with God. They light up from the inside, out. They enjoy life. They're not easily offended. They're enjoyable to be with and they have a sweetness only the Savior could give. They have nothing to prove and only One to please. I love these people! I want to be one of these people! I want to be so saturated with the Savior that people stop and stare. They wonder how can you be so happy, so at peace, so unhindered? Uhhh... Daddy, duh!

That level is possible. It's so special and it comes out of an incredible and intimate life with the Father. An intimacy we will only taste if we will take the time to develop this sweet relationship with Him. He waits for us to come to Him with hearts of desire and longing. To our hearts that anticipate His answer, the Father speaks to us about who we are and who He really is. The Bible tells us that He stands at the door and knocks,

maybe our circumstances are Him knocking
(Revelation 3:20). He's knocking at the door of our
hearts and wanting us to invite Him in. In some
moments it is easier to hear His knock than in
others. Let's be intentional about creating
moments, glimpses even, where we experience
Him deeply.

The Root

root(noun) *the basic cause, source, or origin of something.* "In biology, it is the part of the plant that grows downward and holds the plant in place." Synonyms: established, ingrained, source, origin.[2]

Anxiety comes from one place and one place only, no matter the circumstance that triggers it or the pain that evolves. Anxiety comes from a lack of trust in God. We've all heard, "Trust God," but what does that practically look like and how can we put it to work in our lives? **Focus**. It's easier said than done, but our focus is what navigates our trust. Like a ship on a sea we have to lock eyes with

---

[2] Root. Accessed May 2015 through www.dictionary.com

the lighthouse that leads us safely forward, towards truth.

Anxiety creates a dense fog that covers us so heavily that we cannot see truth, even definite truths we've known our entire lives. When caught in a web of anxiety we can instantly forget truths that are core to our foundation. We can lose sight of all we've been given that stabilizes our soul.

Have you ever experienced such dense fog? I know I have. I have been lost on the emotional rollercoaster of anxiety that feels so real and steals every last string of joy, peace, and sleep from my life. Oh yes, I've ridden the rollercoaster! You've got to get off. That might mean separating yourself from the person, place, or thing causing the anxiety and choosing to get the right perspective. Other times, it means quickly identifying the lies you are believing and powering through.

How did we get here to this tangled place of emotion in our souls? Our enemy works double time when we are young and begins by placing circumstances, people, and weapons he means for our demise in our tracks. Let's not give him too much credit: he's a glorified snake with no teeth. Even still, his sneaky, deceitful plans often cause turmoil and pain that we must address in our lives so that it can be used for good and not evil. We have to revisit our lenses and once again recognize that a loving, all-powerful Father is in control. Nothing that touches our lives has not first passed by Him. It has been acknowledged as a circumstance that will grow us, and ultimately give Him glory.

Since I began my walk with God at the age of 5, the enemy has been on a mission to steal my soul, and he has the same goal in mind for you. He has set up roadblocks, destructive relationships, turmoil and angst. He has tried to convince me that I am bound for failure. Thankfully, our Father is stronger and has a firm hold on us. His Word says *"Do not be afraid for those on our side are more than theirs"* (2 Kings 6:16). We have an army of angels on our side continuing the Father's will of saving our souls by protecting us physically and emotionally. **When all else fails, be convinced of this: you have an army fighting for you!**

The enemy wants us to believe that what we face is so great that it will take us down. But if we know the heart of the Father and trust Him, we know that all we experience in this life is meant to draw us closer to Him. **We can only trust the Father to the level or degree that we experience and allow Him into our lives.** If we see that the pain is there to allow Him to comfort, then we'll see that the fear we experience is meant for Him to show us freedom, and the loss is a way to reveal His love. We will then accept His all-knowing hands and trust Him.

So let's expose the enemy's plans and get to the bottom of what is really going on. To the root. That thing below the surface. Everything has a root. Everything begins somewhere. It has to have a place of beginning. A root is the place where that "thing" began and took up residence in your heart. It's important that we not only recognize something by its root, but also take it out by it's root. We want it all out, even that last little vein of pain that holds on creating darkness. Pull it out! Otherwise that baby will try to grow back.

The root is something that has taken up residence in your core. Roots are organisms that live under the surface. In the depths of the earth and, in this context, the depths of our hearts. Our root system is our belief system; it houses the key memories and habits that we live out daily, without a second thought. For some of us, our roots are healthy. They are full of trust in God and a belief in His power over our lives, but for others of us we have a faulty system, one that was created from broken relationships and times when we felt like God didn't come through on our behalf.

Our core is so incredibly important. We need to take a good hard look at our system and recognize how it got there and what purpose it is serving. Is it life giving and fruitful or is it faulty? How did that root even get in there? It entered by way of a deep and personalized lie that was not exposed upon its entrance. The enemy taunted us with lies and since we were not secure in the Father and His Word, we took his bait. So, we have to search our own hearts and ask the Father to reveal deep things to us.

During this process it's imperative to have ample time alone with the Father. He has to help lead you through this open heart surgery. The beautiful and special part is that the loving Father's desire is to see our hearts made right and drawn closer to Him. He won't deny you if you seek Him and allow Him to heal the broken places in you. Scripture tells us that *"He is close to the broken hearted and binds up their wounds* (Psalm 34:18)." Close. He is so close, both during our healing moments and breaking moments. Often, those are the times He feels farthest but that is a lie of our flesh and the enemy, because Scripture tells us He is close.

In my own personal, painful times of darkness He feels so far, but when I remind myself that He is close, I begin to experience deeper healing and love all around me. I sit in His presence and weep as He purges things out of me. In those moments **He reveals and touches deep places of pain so He can produce purpose.** It's His tender desire to see us live beyond our pain and into His individual purpose for our lives. He's a good Father and as a good Father He doesn't want His children walking around broken, jaded, drained. He wants us to experience on this earth the abundant life He died to give us (John 10:10) What a good Father! What love!

Through pain and purging, I've experienced the Father and His love for me in a way so deep and so tender, I would not have known it had I denied the pain and missed His purpose. He loves us so deeply that He allows pain to call us to Him. We can draw from this depth in times of need.

This depth is only available through intimacy, and intimacy is created in those quiet moments with the Creator of your heart. It's so important to create moments for the Father to meet with us.

Some ways to create those moments:
*weekend getaway with God (my personal fave when available)
*secret room (a room kept sacred because it's only used when spent with "Abba," our Daddy)
*frequent, undisturbed study
*prayer time alone or with 2 or 3 other equally passionate lovers of Abba.
*walks alone or with a close believer

*a nature experience (kayaking, lake, swimming, biking, trail, hiking, fishing, snorkeling, etc)
*serving simply (write cards of encouragement, give gifts, do a special "act of service:" grocery shop for an elderly person, clean, etc.)

In these moments when we spend time alone with the Lord, we begin to experience Him as a loving father. So close, that we can call out and call Him Daddy. For those who have had painful experiences with a father figure, it may be hard at first to see Him as this, but He longs to restore the beauty of that relationship with you. Our Father is the one who can speak life into all the darkness and confusion. He can separate out the truth from the lies. He can revive your heart and make it new.

When I was a child one of my favorite worship songs was "A Pure Heart" by Rusty Nelson. The Song goes like this:

'A pure heart, that's what I long for, a heart that's

undivided after thee. A pure heart that's what I long for, a

heart that follows hard after thee. A heart that hides your

Word, so that sin will not come in. A heart that's

undivided while you rule and reign. A heart that bleeds

compassion and pleases you my Lord. A sweet aroma in

worship, that rises to. Your throne.[3]

The idea of a pure heart was so real to me. I wanted to be pure before God, pure in His presence. Now as an adult it is an incredible desire once again-to be pure in heart before Him.

A pure heart.

Our heart is the keeper of the roots. Those pesky little intruders we described in the beginning diagram as results of insecurity. Insecurity breeds insecurity and what once surfaced as fear, may now look like deep self-loathing. Until we get to the root and remove the deep seated issue, we will be unable to experience healing and live with a pure heart. Therefore to have a pure heart, we have to remove the junk that is clogging our arteries with insecurity.

---

[3] Take the City "A Pure Heart." By Rusty Nelson. CD.

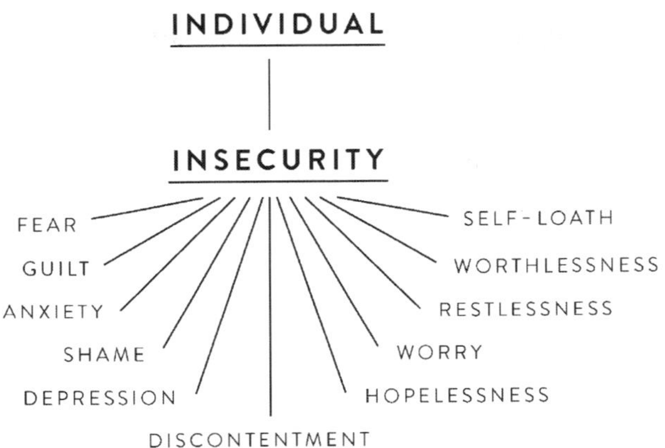

Remember this diagram? If we aren't careful, these little pests can come creeping in. **If we are full of depression, self-loathing, fear, guilt, shame, anxiety and discontentment then an insecure life will be a result.** Living full of regret and fear of the future will automatically create insecurity. We have an army of angels on our side continuing the Father's will of saving our souls by protecting us physically and emotionally. People with anxious hearts cannot rest until they feel accepted and approved.

Not only can insecurity produce all these little roots; but these little roots can produce insecurity.

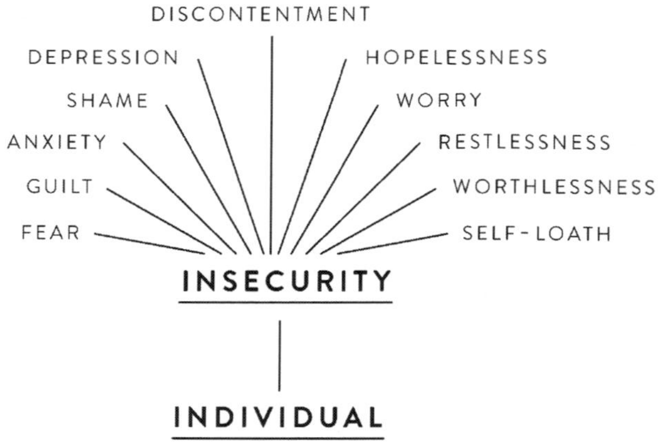

To live unmotivated by these problematic roots we must change our focus (we will talk about this at further length ahead). But **you, and only you can let the Gardener come in and uproot all that has wrongfully taken up residence in your heart.** Whether it came by choice or was put there by another, the Gardener wants to remove its poisonous infestation from your life.

He loves you, let Him in. Let Him change the way you see yourself, the way you see pain, and let Him create purpose in it all. He is a good Father, and He will allow that which was meant for evil to be used for your good and His glory (Genesis 50:20). Let those roots be undone by His love and recreated with His promises. Each root has to be taken out and then replaced by truth. You let the roots in, but only He can take them out. Allow Him to treat each root with His tender Word.

Anxiety comes from the pit of hell...I am absolutely convinced! Not only is it a tool the enemy uses to create monumental distrust in God the Father, but it also feels like a living hell most days. It's painful. Down to our core selves, it sneaks in and steals the peace that Jesus died to give us. Tell me that's not the enemy!

Anxiety can create a deep fear. It is a fear that the bad circumstances will never end and that we have to live as a prisoner to our pain. In my own life, relational pain has caused terrible anxiety, and while that may sound trivial it has been downright debilitating to me at moments. In those moments I get so lost in the lasting pain, that I can't expect change or hope that the future will look any different.

Your world may look different from mine, but I can promise you the remedy is the same. At the lowest moment of my life, Jesus and my close friend were there. I literally had to ask her to pull the car over so I could throw up from the stress and anxiety in my body. I was relying on me. I was questioning, fearing, planning, and chasing. Peace was nowhere to be seen.

The enemy had tricked me into believing it all relied on me -MY world, MY decisions, MY emotions, MY career, and MY relationships. The weight of the world fell on my shoulders and I couldn't breathe. Anxiety churned in my spirit and swirled in my stomach. Let me take a moment and say, do not feel guilty for the physical responses that take place in your body! Nausea, redness, shakes, hives… these are all reactions that your body creates. Our body was made to respond to fears to keep us safe. Whether a perceived fear or real, a response will take place. You can't override this. Work on identifying the root (what causes it) and these symptoms will minimize and eventually vanish.

Scripture promises healing; that means it's yours. Jesus died to give you this. Believe it and soon you'll see the fruit of His labor as He replaces the seeds of fear with faith. Let's be people who recognize seeds of destruction and lies, uproot them, and replace them with Jesus' life.

How does this happen? Getting to the root(s) is not often easy. It requires self-evaluation, a substantial amount of time with the Holy Spirit, journaling, prayer, and sometimes seasons of fasting. The Lord wants to reveal the things that are causing pain in your life that He did not put there. To move forward, we have to look back, not to stay there, but to gain insight. Then, we can take steps toward the freedom we have in Christ.

What causes fear in your heart?

Why?

Can you remember the first time you felt this fear?

Knowing this information can help you reveal where the wound entered, and go to that place with the Lord and seek healing. He desires to restore you, to bring you to a place where you are no longer bound by fear, but rather, restored to a place of freedom and peace. When we journey with Jesus, we can be restored to our default setting of peace and trusting God (remember how free you were as a child?), and by abiding in Jesus we can find ourselves even better off than we began.

Living life in freedom is possible!

Smooth Trail or A Derail?

I love to hike. I love walking a path that is almost completely engulfed in nature, in the middle of lush, green woods, barely traceable to the common eye. An uncharted trail is so exciting, so invigorating! All you need is the peace and security of knowing that it leads somewhere, that it is safe, and off you can go.

God leads us along those kinds of paths, paths that produce peace, and disperse any angst. He leads us to places of promise, even if it is through places of pain. We trust Him because the trail is right; it settles peacefully and securely in our hearts.

Satan leads us on trails meant to derail. He shows us ways to lose our focus, misplace our trust, and disregard/disrupt our faith. He creates paths that look "pretty" or "promising", but steal our peace and security. He does it in such a way that confuses us and causes us to question ourselves. Where he can create confusion and stress, he brings us the opportunity to take the bait and experience anxiety and panic.

Things that seem "good" may be disguised to derail our purpose. Even ministry, relationships, and godly functions can be used to disrupt your peace and take you off the special path God has for you (which often is the cause of angst). You know it isn't right, but you settle in that it's a "good" thing or "noble," so it must be God. What a ploy! He knows he can't steal our salvation, so he'll squander our peace and make us miserable by running after the wrong things, all the while plagued as we search for purpose.

Well played enemy, well played, but this generation is smarter than that and we have a Father who loves us and won't let us go too far. Have you ever continued on a derailed path and experienced anxiety? Sometimes our "inner alarm" is correct and it is warning us that we've gotten on a wrong path and aren't living the life we were meant to live.

What does a derailed path look like? Here's an example: Your cousin Emily sets you up on a date with John. He's sweet, loves Jesus, and wants to be a missionary. You have no real connection with him and he doesn't really fit what you believe God has for your future...but Emily and your whole family think he's incredible. So, you push past all the red flags and silent nudges. Six months later you find yourself derailed. You are anxious, unnervingly worried about the future, and uncertain about what God has called you to be...why? Because you silenced the still small voice and amplified the voices of those around you.

Or, how about the ministry opportunity you took? You felt guilted into it and uneasy, but just chalked that up to an overworked self or a fleshly imagination. Then, a year later, you're sitting in the living room asking yourself why you are miserable and questioning why you let it get this far. How can you be so unhappy doing such a "good thing?"

You've been derailed, my friend.

Wow! It's not easily detected and it's really smart on our enemy's part. He knows if he were to use something that trips our circuit and sends an alarm, he'd be caught. So he's gotten creative. For those of us who choose to follow God and the incredible plans He has for us, we can be sure our enemy will be close behind creating distractions and opportunities for angst in our souls.

If we were willing to give up and give in to the pressures of life and just "be normal," we would probably not experience such painful push backs from the enemy. He would still try attacking us in hopes of hurting our most precious relationship, our relationship with Christ, but were we to forfeit our purposes for a path easier to tread he would be sufficiently happy.

This week even in the midst of incredible spiritual growth and a renewed desire for God's Word, I find myself tempted by potential derails. Good ones. Fun ones. Seriously stinking awesome ones! Those who know me, know that I can't turn down a party, but in the depths of my soul I know it's more distractions meant to work against my purpose. We need to have narrow focuses to obtain and retain our peace, to live the well meaning life God has for us, full of passion and void of distraction.

How do we get so easily distracted? It's easy. We look around and observe the needs of others and the neediness of our own hearts for love and admiration. We know that if we continue to say yes and impress people with our love, we will fill our empty banks. Other times, it's an easier answer. We just want to have fun and enjoy life, but God's kingdom is all about balance. I, like Paul, have not reached that place of perfection, but I see the goal and I try to live with it before me (Philippians 3:12). Although it often involves letting others down, the purposeful lives God has for us are laser focused. **They understand their true purpose and pursuit and live vigorously to accomplish just that!**

Most people find it incredibly painful to live lives that are not concentrated on people pleasing, but, on purpose. It's difficult. We are meant to live lives that serve one another, but not lives that sacrifice God's desires for us in the hopes of pleasing another…it's a fine line in our minds, but it's boldly different to God. I can quickly fill my week's schedule with things that make my brother or sister happy, but don't fulfill my purpose or passions one time that week. The person who is benefiting can be happy for a very short period of time while you're babysitting, when you run that errand, or while you're at that Bible study but **in the long run everyone is happier when we're each fulfilling our purpose!**

Life really looks like a myriad of choices. Each choice leads us closer to or away from our purpose. These choices create overall joy or questioning confusion in our minds and hearts. I've gotten off track at times and taken a path not designated for me. It sucks! We really are created with a specific purpose in mind.

By getting sidetracked, I get confused and the questions start rolling in. Am I where I'm supposed to be? Why am I not fulfilled? Should I be doing something different? We feel like we can't tell up from down. If only we can keep our lives and ourselves consecrated, we will live purposeful lives of intentionality.

I don't know about you, but I think a life full of passion and purpose sounds amazing. Billy Graham comes to mind. A saint so fulfilled in his purpose. That's what I want! A life of passion! Have you met people who live like this? They are fun, they are happy, they are hopeful, and it's because they are living lives on point. This makes me think of Jesus' words in Matthew 22:14 *"Many are called, but few are chosen"*. Many are given callings, few pursue them. Few live them. Few experience that joy. **I want to be one of the few!**

In choosing to be a few, be careful not to run ahead of God. Some of us have received the vision, but we're waiting on the Father's timing.

Wait. Trust that He knows when and what's best. His plans for our individual lives are so good! I'm so thankful that He loves us all as His children and as His individual kids. He's such a great Dad!

So, once you know Dad's perfect plan for you, (which comes in pieces, not in total picture form), run towards it, with passion and purpose! If He's given you a heart for a specific thing, seek and serve in that wholeheartedly and let Him show you the rest. **He's a good Father, who gives good gifts. Trust that the purpose or dream He gives you will bring joy to your heart and serve His ultimate plan.** He leads you down specific paths meant for your growth that create opportunities for you to more intimately know the Father. Let Him lead you there.

Sometimes it's hard to just enjoy the lives He's given us, but our Father wants us to. He wants us to have and enjoy our lives (John 10:10). Don't be so serious! Easier said than done I know, but it would incredibly improve our lives. **How much more enjoyable would life be if we just enjoyed it?** (Such a crazy concept!).

Life from our Father is a gift. He loves us and desires us to enjoy all that He has given us. We have been given incredible and precious gifts of opportunity, friendships, loved ones, and divine relationships through our churches and jobs. God has given us all we need for life and godliness (2 Peter 1:3). We can live lives that truly glorify God and experience His blessing and favor in life.

Sometimes in order to fully enjoy the life God has for us, we need to take moments to disconnect from all the chaos and connect with our Creator. Maybe that means leaving work early to go take a walk and talk with God, or embracing your creative side while painting pottery, or maybe it's simply spending some alone time relaxing with a favorite movie. It's important that we learn to experience God in the everyday. To enjoy all that He's given us and connect with Him in every area of our lives. That's what a rich life looks like. That is a trail well walked and enjoyed. One that brings joy to every area-mind, body, soul and spirit. Every area of our inner man, (mind, body, soul and spirit), enjoying all we've been given- that's good stuff.

January 6,2016

"There have been emotional and tough moments, but I know remaining steadfast even with these emotions is best...God, please continue to show me how. The way."

Tough days will come. It's important to choose before they come how you will react.

I wrote the above journal entry during one of my dark moments. I had to decide to remember the importance of steadfastness, a lesson God continues to deepen within me. What repeating words or patterns do you see God weaving into your life? As they come, tuck them away for future use.

"Choose this day, whom you will serve..."
Joshua 24:15

Once you've chosen, give it all you've got! A trail is not always promised to be easy. Heck, trails aren't always marked! Trails have bumps, detours, ups and downs. They are beautiful and there are spots where you get dirty, or fall into a hole. Sometimes you go at a trail alone and sometimes company is best. But one thing is for sure, when walking a trail you always need to be wearing the right gear-shoes, layers, lack of layers, maybe a hat... You need water and a protein bar or two. When you walk a trail or ride a trail, you prepare for anything.

This is where the full armor of God comes in. Every piece is crucial. It protects us, prepares us to be offensive or defensive, and even to deal with things we can't see. Each piece creates a protective layer over key areas such as our hearts, minds, and vital organs. The right gear is imperative, whether on a physical trail or a spiritual one.

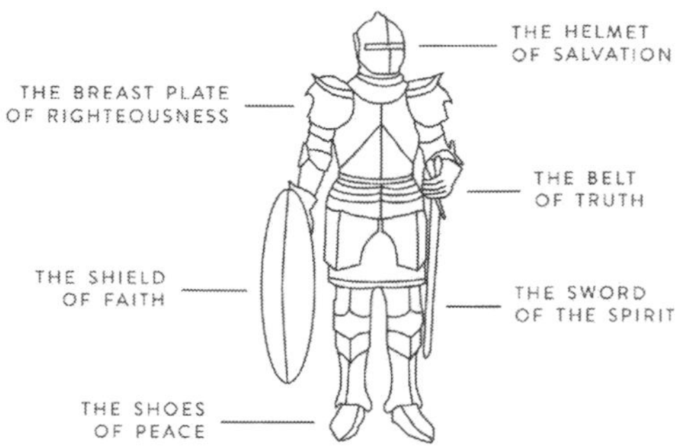

With each piece of spiritual armor on, we can decipher if this is a smooth trail, or a derailing one. Our spiritual armor helps us to test and approve, and in that we experience God's will (Romans 12:2). We've been given the tools.

That's what we have to remember when we take a trail in our lives. We know we are walking with Jesus, so we're secure. We can stay on the trail and not get derailed. We can lean in and enjoy the trail, even without knowing the exact destination. Our only agenda is to take in the scenery, learn the lessons, and gain the tools. The trail is training. So grab your tools and let's get to walking friends!

You've got it!

I've got it!

We've been set up for success!

Call It What It Is

*The thief comes to steal, kill and destroy, but I
have come that they may have life more abundantly.*
- John 10:10

Steal. Kill. Destroy. I don't know about
you, but that motto has played out in my life so
many times and in so many ways. Relationships,
jobs, thoughts, actions, my own sinfulness… steal,
kill, destroy. I've allowed my flesh to do it to me
and the enemy of my soul to, as well.

Have you ever had literal thoughts of death.
"I want to die right now!" Or sat in the darkness of
depression for days wondering why? Have you ever
been so emotionally broken that one more thing
would literally break you to pieces? Death. He
wants to kill you!

So much of our healing comes in recognizing and calling things as they are! Depressing thoughts, damaging relationships, dreaded dreams...Kill! Steal! Destroy! It's the message from a murderous enemy. One who wants nothing more than to **destroy your destiny**. If all hell is breaking loose and you think you are about to lose it, **be of good cheer- for you are chosen!** The fact that the enemy is against you means you were marked for greatness.

In my own life it's often been so hard to decipher what is happening at times; why I'm responding to things out of hurt and why all these painful circumstances are culminating in my life? Then when I feel the darkness all around and the cords of death around my neck, I can recognize that **it's an assignment to take me out.** It's the plans of my enemy.

Oh, how angry and ready to kick some devil butt that makes me! It makes me want to get to fighting, living, and making my enemy wish he didn't mess with me. **Because the fact that he tries, is evidence of the truth that I'm called by Jesus for big things!** That alone puts motion to my feet and a message in my mouth.

Whether a small attack, a big distraction, or a painful memory- the enemy has one goal - my demise. And he's going to fight to take me out.

The thing is, it's not just me. Maybe you think your wild thoughts are your fault or a product of your imagination. Maybe you see yourself as lazy, but that's a lie the enemy used someone's voice to speak over you as a child. Maybe you feel unloved and often respond from a broken heart. Here, your actions can be attributed to a seed planted by the deceiver. But you don't have to stay there, and neither do I. We can gain insight and allow God to defeat our foe through His Word and our faithfulness in believing it.

The enemy is going to have to use new tactics and fight even dirtier, because I'm gaining strength and knowledge, and so can you! Those are two things that will take down his kingdom and evil plans for me, quickly and with great precision. Like a daughter of the King wielding a mighty sword. In Jesus' name, I am a spiritual force to be reckoned with.

Call it "targeted", call it "sought after", or call it "stalked" - I call it chosen. And if you and I weren't chosen, the enemy wouldn't waste his time trying to take us out. So stand strong. Stand bold. Stand ready. You're called! You're chosen! You have a mission! It's for real. Get ready!

Beauty
I didn't want to have to deal with the deeper things today but that was Your plan. The closer I get to You God, the more sensitive I become. Father, I'm beginning to really get it. Your power is greater! It's greater than my pain. It's greater than the mistakes I've made and the sin I've committed-your blood is greater! I choose to really believe that! You see the greatness You planted in me, and so does the enemy and he wants me to give up and let go of the promise. But I've tasted and seen that You are good Jesus! God, I'm really just beginning to get a clear picture of what Jesus did on the cross for me. Thank you!
*A Personal Journal entry

The enemy constantly wants us to be discouraged in our relationship with Jesus. He wants us to get off track, disconnected, and ashamed by our lack of connection. Curled up in the fetal position, afraid to move forward, withdrawn for fear of what lies ahead. ***No stinking way!!*** That's so the opposite of what Jesus meant when He promised us "abundant life" in Scripture. If what you feel, sense, and are experiencing does not sound like the truth of Scripture-it's not the promised, powerful, and purposed life Jesus died to give you.

Journal out some of your days, and if you see the destructive fingerprint of the enemy

themed through it, call that stuff out! Some days I
see division, anxiety, brokenness, and pain-yikes!
Not today, Satan! I'm going to live the life my
Father has for me! Serving others, loving deeply,
and freely embracing each day!

If you are, like me, often plagued by the
enemy's tactics, get ready! Because when freedom
begins to take root will you get a holy boldness that
all of hell cannot fight! Get excited! You're on the
winning side! The Bible says *"no weapon formed
against you will prosper"* (Isaiah 54:17) and I like to
believe, in my righteous anger, that God takes that
very weapon and uses it to bring about His glory
and the enemies further demise! (I'm one of those
chicks who wants to put on boxing gloves and
sucker punch the enemy for all the junk he's put me
through, and the ways he's disillusioned God's
people.) - "It's on like Donkey Kong!" (I'm such a
90s kid).

If I could name every child of God that has
been plagued with anxiety I would spend the day
rehearsing. It's an abomination to our faith. A
poison to our souls, and a destroyer of
relationships and destinies. It makes me so angry!
With each pain of anxiety, he's quick to leave a trail
of memories that flash back at the most
inopportune times. Surfacing in our souls and
squandering our joy and peace. It's downright

annoying and debilitating! The insecurity this deadly poison creates is draining the very life out of us. It's time to call that stuff out and take it to the Father!

The Pain You Feel Is Real

Taking a plain look at your pain and recognizing it as valid is a HUGE step in moving forward to be the person God has called you to be. Maybe it's a fear that God isn't real, that's valid. Many people struggle with questions and security revolving around their relationship with Christ. But you can have security. Maybe you were in a horrible relationship and now being with the opposite sex is a bit frightening, and you wonder if you will ever get married or love again. That's valid, that's real. But God does want to heal that broken place. Maybe your last job was an absolute nightmare, everything fell apart and you were left moving back to your hometown in search of peace. Now, you are terrified to try again. What happens if I fail again, or worse? I can't do that pain. That is valid. Fear of failure is the underlying cause of many of our most painful reluctances as human beings. But God has big plans for you and your life is going to count for something amazing, so get ready to experience healing!

Allow yourself to grieve. It's so important, and is healthy and crucial to your overall healing. Without truly grieving the loss, disappointment, expectations and painful experiences, we cannot truly begin to move forward. Accepting our reality is key to experiencing wholeness. **I cannot move past what I do not accept.**

Choose to be present in that reality but expectant of greater things! Have a picture of what healthy and thriving could mean in your life. You have the opportunity to take that thing, that place of pain and use it for purpose. What would that look like?

Living as though a painful experience did not take place is easier, but continuing to live as though nothing happened to us may ease tension temporarily, but will prove to be painful poison tearing at the inside of the core of who we are. An inner war will eventually take place, and when it does it will be reality colliding with the imaginary life we've created to keep ourselves safe. Survival is not worth freedom and the opportunity to truly live.

Personally, I have chosen to live in that world, sometimes for extended periods of time, but much like a person with cancer is not cured just because they pretend the disease is not present, I cannot be "cured" or healed from the painful disease eating away at my very being if I don't address it.

Sometimes we don't address it because our thoughts are so unhealthy that they take us to places of despair, angst, and darkness that we should never have to deal with. Other times it's unconfessed sin in our lives eating away at us. And then there are times when we don't address a boundary issue and we aren't protecting our property (from expectations, demands, others, schedules that drain, painful thoughts).

Boundaries are often incredibly hard to define and if we are people-pleasers, even in the purest form, it can be a painful creation. I tend to be that person in many relationships and ministries who says yes to helping others, or "pleasing" others, but then pays for it with my own lack of peace and enjoyment. Our Father does not long for that for us, that's why even Jesus had to create healthy boundaries. He had to sneak away,

He had to tell people no, and He had to be true to His identity and calling. That's how **His focus was clear and His peace was held.**

In their book *Boundaries*, Cloud and Townsend refer to the greatest commandment given by Jesus in Matthew 22:37-40, which is to,

> *"love the Lord your God with all your heart and with all your soul and with all your mind. This is the first and greatest commandment. And the second is like it: Love your neighbor as yourself. All the Law and the Prophets hang on these two commandments"* (Matthew 22:40).

"But how do we do that? Well, that's why there are so many other passages! Loving God and our neighbor is difficult. One of the main reasons it's so difficult is because of boundary problems, which are essentially problems of responsibility. We do not know who is responsible for what, where we end and someone else begins, or where God ends and we begin. The Bible clarifies those boundaries so that we can begin to see who should do what in this labor of love[4]."

---

[4] Cloud, Henry and John Townsend. Boundaries: When to Say Yes, When to Say No, to Take Control of Your Life. Zondervan, 2017.

God has created us with boundaries because He Himself operates with them. When we define and operate in our healthy boundaries, we experience peace at another level. We are not worried about man's approval or others disdain, we are free to be ourselves and live life in that peace. Our choice to live with boundaries will help us experience peace and the soothing comfort Jesus desires to give us in the midst of life's demands and pain.

Your pain is real, but it is meant to point you to the Healer. Pain is created in the context of relationships and can only truly be healed in a relationship with the One who created you and knows you best. He desires to reveal His love for you as you accept the challenges and difficulties of this life. **If you ignore the pain, you might miss His purpose.** The same comfort He is wanting to give you, He is wanting to give to others through you (2 Cor. 1:34). So let Him love you and then use that redeeming love to show others the powerful hand at work in your life.

The Psalmist, David, wrote *"When anxiety was great within me, your consolation brought me joy"* (Psalm 94:29). His comfort, His consolation is the only thing that can soothe the anxiety deep within us. Yet to experience that consolation we must describe the pain within our souls to our Divine

Healer. Psalm 18:6 says *"In my distress I called to the Lord; I cried to my God for help. From his temple he heard my voice; my cry came before him, into his ears. Only He knows what to do and how to do it."* **Only He can take our pain and create His purpose.** So respond child of God. Answer the deep groans of your anguished soul with a BOLD determination to seek the Father's face.

4/13/2015

"God, it is so easy to identify the enemy's little foxes trying to get in the vineyard. As I continue to do battle I am able to see more clearly that God has so much for me and my enemy wants to stop me. My enemy wants the little foxes to eat the entire vineyard. No WAY!
My whole life is about God!
My whole life belongs to You!
The lame, lying enemy wants me to step back and be scared. The dreams make me feel so timid. They make me lose some of my boldness. NOT SO! I'm filled with the Holy Spirit! The enemy's ultimate goal is to silence me.
NOT SO!"

My own personal faith walk is hard. That's a look into my life. **We can't heal what we don't uncover.** The enemy works so hard to silence us. So fiercely. So below the belt. But when you see the skin of the snake, you know he's been there, sneaking around on his belly. Squirming and making lame attempts to bring you down with him. Resist him and he will flee! (James 4:7).

October 13, 2014

"Wow, my journal entries could read like the Psalms of David. After the start of a new high, a first in a long time, I've crashed…my emotions derailing, anxious and afraid about my future and angry that I'm afraid. Feeling like giving up on God and living my own life, that would make me happy. I had done some self talk but I feel like I came home and got back into the rut, old habits. Worrying about my job, career, future, calling, family, etc and even small things…it makes me so angry at me: why can't I be confident in decisions? Why do I second guess myself so much? Why do I worry? Why can't I live in your peace?"

October 14, 2014

"I don't even know where to begin with writing about this inner struggle. It's so painful. I feel so void. Like I just want to give up. I need peace."

The struggle is real. But our focus is crucial. I lost focus in these moments and the enemy smirked. It looked like he was winning, and sometimes it still does from the outside, but God is on my side. **His truth will set you free!** If you feel surrounded by guilt and claustrophobia then speak

"God has set my feet in a <u>spacious</u> place!" (Psalm 18:19). From personal experience, I know it can be so hard to stop the thoughts or speak out loud. Even still, you have to begin to try and take that territory back. Your mind really is the battleground, and you have to win the hardest fights of life on that field. Dig in your heels and stare down those big offenders coming at you. You've got killer armor and a regiment of angels behind you.

It will take time, and there will be times when you lose battles, but *take heart for He has overcome the world* (John 16:33). Allow the promises found in His Word to seal freedom in the depth of your soul. See your pain as an invitation to come. Just as you are. Shakey, scared, annoyed, frustrated, broken....He isn't afraid of what you feel. Really. He's felt it and He invites you to meet Him there. In the midst of the madness. See Him there. **Your pain is not greater than the promise He has for you.** Press on friend.

The Blasted P Word!

"You gain strength, courage and confidence by every experience in which you really stop to look fear in the face. You must do the thing which you think you cannot do."
-Eleanor Roosevelt

I hate words that begin with P. Pain. Panties. Pimple. Panic. The list gets worse, so I'll stop, but my least favorite P word of all time is <u>process</u>. Just the word alone makes me say-are you freaking kidding me?! I want to slam my hands on the table, push my chair back, and walk away in absolute disgrace that anyone would expect me to endure something for a long time- hell no! Life is hard enough!

But, I serve a Master who makes a message out of the journey, the process. The daily grind. The weekly battle. The monthly counseling session. All the while chipping away at our less than perfect frame, and making us more like Jesus.

Michelangelo'd

When Michelangelo created David from one large block of marble, he was asked how he created such a masterpiece. His response was simple. *"All I did was chip away everything that didn't look like David."* Little by little, the artist chipped away at all that was not David and created an impressive masterpiece that has stood the test of time, leaving generations intrigued and astonished.

During a deep season of process, the Lord used that story to speak to me and the term "Michaelangelo'd" was born.

Michaelangelo'd, we are! Thank God! Little by little, He is shaping our attitudes, actions and attributes, until we reflect the likeness of Christ. *"We all with unveiled faces contemplate/reflect the Lord's glory, are being transformed into His image with ever-increasing glory, which comes from the Lord, who is the Spirit"* (2 Corinthians 3:18). He's changing us daily, whether we realize it or not. If we've agreed to be His kids and submitted to the process, He's shaping us. He's doing a work within us that will produce "eternal glory." Results we can't even begin to imagine, because again, it's not about us it's about Him.

I literally feel like my life has been one giant process. Pain, challenges, growth, work, and back to pain. Yet in it all, I have been shaped. A sweet friend of mine reminded me during trying hours that God was preparing me. He was using my affliction/my tests to confirm in me and prepare me for what was next; to check off completion and growth in an area so I could move on to what He has for me next. Kind of like that fun fable that says don't pray for patience, because then the Lord will teach you to be patient. It's no joke. You signed up for a long lesson in growing, dear friend.

As I sit here today, I am amused at the "process" the Lord has used to bring me to where I am and make me who I am meant to be, **in this moment.** A year ago my life was entirely different. The Lord used so many things, including a back break (yeah, you read that right) to get me to where He needed me to be. Now, He didn't cause it, but He sure as heck used it my friend. He will use anything you allow Him to, in order to speak to you. There is a point to the process. Ultimately, it's holiness, but the baby steps are all along the way.

The process of brokenness.

I referred earlier to a season where God literally stripped everything away out of my life. I was living a simple life as a nanny, in a new town, counseling through some past pains, in debt, and happy as a clam in a cute little place all my own. One day I was working and started having sharp pain in my stomach and feeling dizzy, which I had never experienced. I'm a pain silencer, so I kept going and took the kids out for the day (More on pain silencing later). The next few days the pain got worse, until one night/morning at 5am, I realized I needed to go to the hospital and did. The long and short of it was that in my younger years, probably high school sports, I had incurred two fractures in my back and the disc between them had dissolved.

Pain. No joke.

It had stayed silent all these years but with taking on additional weight and carrying two babies daily, it started to scream at me. But with all that, I couldn't carry the kids, therefore no more nannying. I had to move home with my parents to be taken care of for months. While home, the relationship I was in ended and I started working for a new company. So many major things took place in a short period of time and I was broken.

Literally and emotionally. I'm a strong woman, but I found myself crying sometimes and not even knowing why, but the Lord was working. This was all part of my process. He was making me into a more tender woman in the role He had called me to, and in doing so, He re-established me with my family. **The hurt was leading to healing.** A.W. Tozer said *"When I understand that everything happening to me is to make me more Christlike, it resolves a great deal of anxiety."*

Now to pain silencing. Friends, not only is that physically possible, that is sure as heck, emotionally and spiritually possible. It's possible to avoid pain for a long time, but just like my back, the pain will come up at the most inopportune time. That's why the Father longs to bring healing. He longs to hold your hand and walk you back through the pain and into freedom. Yes, the emotions will come up at times and be so very hard, but He won't leave you. Trust the process.

The process of peace.

Peace is something we are promised as God's kids, but sometimes it can feel like we are walking around in the dark, bumping into walls, looking for it. Why? Often it exists the greatest in His will, and that is definitely a process to find. I like to think about it like this, we will always have God's peace as His kids, but there is a bullseye He's leading us to. Like you can have peace everywhere, but that thing will be deep and tangible where He's leading.

**I want the greatest peace possible.
I want to live in that.**
Don't you?

In Colossians 3:15 in the AMPC version it says *"and let the peace (soul harmony which comes) from Christ rule (act as an **umpire** continually) in your hearts [deciding and settling with finality all questions that arise in your minds, in that peaceful state] to which as [members of Christ's] one body you were also called [to live]. And be thankful (appreciative), [giving praise to God always]."*

An umpire. He's the guy who yells "safe" or "out" at a baseball game. That's the type of rule peace is supposed to have in our lives. No peace? "Out!" Peace? "Safe!" That's an easy judge where you can discern what peace is like. But what if you can't?

Peace is defined by Webster's dictionary as:
1. A state of tranquility or quiet.

2. Freedom from disquieting or oppressive thoughts or emotions.
3. Harmony in personal relations.

In the New Testament, the word for peace is *eirene* in Greek, and speaks of rest and tranquility.

Does your life reflect this state? Is peace ruling in your heart? Acting as an umpire. Let's only hit a few walls, brothers and sisters, as we search for this precious gift. It's a promise from Daddy. Take hold of peace while you're in the process.

Sometimes the enemy has a truer image of us than we do, which is why he is terrified, but don't give him opportunity to torment you with fear. Be bold. Be strong. His fear should give you greater boldness. It's a process, be patient with yourself and pursue peace. The Father has big plans ahead, and to be the best, healthiest, freest version of yourself, you have to allow Him to take you through the process.

When your enemy attempts to take your peace, it's because he's well aware of your purpose.

My life has often reflected this truth. After being in an abusive, romantic relationship, my mind and my enemy reminded me of the pain in each relationship I entered after. The enemy would literally tell me and cause me to believe, that I would never be able to experience real love. That I was truly so broken that it would be impossible to ever experience healing and have a healthy marriage or children.

Sadly, I fell hook line and sinker, because my past was my point of reference. It was what I used to define and project onto the future. <u>But</u>, peace was my promise and peace is YOURS. As God's kids, we are promised peace. We're promised blessing, and we're promised fruitfulness. I couldn't receive these things fully, because my belief was based on my background, not my God's faithfulness.

Wow.

It's all part of the process, and part of the process will definitely require rewriting your belief system. It will require days of digging into the Word and replacing deep seated lies that have taken hold for too long. Once you get that stuff out, then you will enter into a process of putting good stuff (truth) in. Put on your seat belt friend, it's a process, but you'll be so glad you endured in the end.

Looking up, not in

Anxiety has a pretentious way of causing us to look in and not up. Have you ever noticed that when you are anxious you tend to be consumed with your own thoughts, fears, safety, and life? You retreat from being social to introverted, and from serving to surviving. What a keen and crafty way for the enemy of our souls to get us distracted and off track from the things of God. Let's remember that scripture tells us the serpent was more *cunning* than all the other creatures the Lord had made (Genesis 3:1). He's got some experience in this. In manipulation, deceit, and murder. So do not be surprised if you are one of his chosen victims, it just means you are a true child of God and called to big things! Chosen in more ways than one!

The enemy can smell the anointing from a mile away and many times if the first situation he tried did not accomplish his goal, he will try something new he believes can succeed in his ultimate plan: your death.

Journal entry- January 2, 2016

"There's been this inner war in me for as long as I can remember. This tangled up, ugly thing, bitterly fighting for rule inside of me. It's almost if I have always been able to physically feel the spiritual battle that is going on for my soul. The fight of my life. It's been a battle from start to finish. Moments where I can feel Jesus calling me and see His loving hand reaching out, then an unseen enemy sneaks in and tortures my thoughts creating confusion and distress in my body. When will this war end? Is it only in my imagination because I feel it within, like the tumultuous waves of the sea. Rising and falling back in place. Lasting rest, my greatest desire. Lasting rest in the arms of the Father. That sounds a lot like death, freedom from this body and unity with God. Fighting for truth. Fighting for freedom. Fighting for love. Because in the end-love wins."

Can somebody say Psalm? Woah! That there is a roller coaster of an emotional journey, and insanely real. It's a fight for survival some days and a balancing act on others. Everything around us warring for our attention.

The thing is, I have a choice. You have a choice. If we choose to look up and not in, we can live in incredible victory and experience a fulfilling, powerful life, one that slaps the enemy in his silly little face. But it takes locked focus and precise planning. Strategy. A better strategy than his. Eyes on the prize. An undying loyalty to Daddy that makes us indestructible based on our connection with Jesus. Undeniable in our affection and affirmation, and unstoppable in our cause for Christ! Choose to use what the enemy is trying to use to distract you as a tool to point to the Father. If he's causing distrust in others and offense, study love and pray for it. **Pursue the place he's trying to bring pain and confusion to, <u>because there is a reason for it</u>.** He wants you to miss out on all God has for you, in that place.

Ironically, while writing this chapter I received a call from a friend, anxious and in a frenzy. Irrational and scared. Her life is in what seems to her as shambles, and the enemy is in momentary joyful zeal. Yet as she begins to tell me what has just taken place I have to immediately stop her and say "You are anointed and called, and your enemy wants to kill you. The first few tries have not worked, so he's trying again." It may sound dramatic, but it is not. It is the God's honest truth found in His Word. That's not meant to scare you but to create a holy passion inside of you that will help you to live boldly.

John 10:10 *"The thief comes only to <u>steal and kill and destroy</u>;* **I have come that they may have life, and have it to the full."**

Her life began with a painful childhood and dysfunctional systems, and is currently spiraling on a broken axis due to a new circumstance. Yet, the key is her perspective.

To experience success in her story, her future is dependant on her perspective. Will she see all these "isolated events" as a chain potentate of poison from her enemy or believe that she is alone fighting people, places, and things? The potent is a cruel killer and will begin to erode our lives if we continue to ingest it.

If we can purpose ourselves to look up, to look up to the hills from where our help comes from (Psalm 121:1); we can begin to experience healing and receive a new perspective. Until we can break free of these emotions and cycles from our enemy, we cannot regain our ground. God has **promised** us every spiritual blessing. It's ours! No assembly required, but the enemy of our souls will try his best to block and safeguard us from receiving those blessings.

Again, this is where the full armor of God comes in. Literally, putting it on daily. The battles are not to receive things from God. It's to gain and keep those things He's given us and not allow our enemy to deceive us in making us believe they are not ours. God has given us His truth, but we must fight to maintain peace.

The entire armor must be worn daily to fend off any arrows the enemy may try to use to penetrate our mind, soul, heart, and spirit in order to kill us. He gets creative when he recognizes an area in our lives is not being conquered or achieving his goals, so he tries another. It's crucial to our survival and God given thriving life that we suit up daily!

Life will give us pain and problems but if we will allow them, they will ignite our potential!

Each of us knows the pain of rejection, failure, and opposition, but God created those things to stimulate our growth and bring about greater change. Often we plan our lives and situations come along that "derail us," but if we will open our eyes to the all knowing Father who is always at work, He may just cause that thing to bring about our healing or reveal the exact purpose He placed us on this earth for.

Pain has the potential to produce so much in us if we will allow transformation to take place.

Joseph in Scripture went through real, raw, painful experiences and yet those experiences led him straight into his destiny and ultimately his calling, to save his people from famine. Joseph is not a superhero. Those opportunities warranted him the same opportunities and options our trials do: to become bitter, resentful, unforgiving, angry, etc.; or to stay pure before the Lord and allow God's ultimate purpose to prevail. Just think of what He can do through you if you allow yourself to see each trial as a refining tool and not a means for your demise.

"The enemy meant it for evil, <u>but God</u> brought it about for good" (Genesis 50:20). All the tools the enemy has tried to use for our destruction can be used by the lover of our soul to advance His Kingdom. What an awesome way to crush the serpent's head under our feet! Woohoo! Let's take his painful attempts to defeat us and use them for the glory of God!

Our anxiety tries to take away our voice but there are many scriptures that invite us to cry to the Lord in our distress and He will hear us and save us, deliver us, answer us, comfort us, shelter us, rescue us, restore us, and give us favor. When anxiety strikes we have the opportunity to choose self-protection and turn inward, or to look to the Father and allow Him to speak to the deepest places of our hearts.

When you have time, take a few minutes and read these verses. They are promises to rest in.

Job 5:8	Psalm 50:15	Isaiah 5:8
Psalm 18:16	Psalm 81:7	Isaiah 30:19
Psalm 20:1	Psalm 77:2	Isaiah 58:19
Job 33:26	Psalm 86:7	Jer. 29:12
Psalm 27:5	Psalm 107:6	Jer. 33:3
Psalm 22:23	Psalm 107:13	Jer. 39:17

Do you know what each of these verses are? They are an altar. An altar built to remember where God has brought the writer and what He led them out of. In the Old Testament, the believers were taught to build altars as a place of remembrance. Remembrance of deliverance, provision, or a supernatural meeting. A place whether physical or emotional in nature, where God met man and met his needs in a divine way.

Today, more than ever, we need altars of remembrance. We need to look back and remember where God has brought us from and how He has moved in our lives, so that we can trust Him with our future. Our altars can help us to look up and not in. When we focus on what God has done in the past, we can believe Him to do great things in the future.

Our "issues," our "challenges," the "anxieties" of life, are meant to draw us to the loving Father who will give us the attitude and attributes we need to receive from Him and then use our restored voice to declare His praises. Once we have looked up and received what He has for us, we can then praise Him as He sets us free.

After being silenced by anxiety and painful voices, I turned to God and implemented the wisdom given by His Word, which gave me the strength to fight. I have now regained my voice and in regaining my voice I am passionate about helping others in the dark, acquire freedom. **This generation is anointed and called by God to do great things!** The enemy is so scared of us that he is adamant about trying to detour and destroy us and the mission of reaching all with the gospel and love of Jesus Christ.

It's our responsibility to get serious about looking up to the Father who is ready and willing, but we have to change our perspective. We have to get the right view in all of this. It's easy for anxiety to grip us and shut us down, but as your friend viewing it from the outside I can see his master plan- *silence*. Anxiety silences us as a protective mechanism and causes solid believers to be silent survivors. Christ's plan is the opposite. He desires for us to be vocal victors. Proclaiming His love and truth to a lost generation.

But unless we gain purposed perspective (a real relationship and focus on Christ), we will be knocked around by the waves of adversity and anxiety. When the waves come, even the most sincere follower of Christ can get knocked around, therefore it is imperative that we focus on Jesus, use our voice and call out to Him, and surround ourselves with other strong believers. In moments of anxiety the fog is so dense, you can't see clearly and you can't shut off your brain-but you have to silence the noise and sneak away with the Father. **If you don't retreat with Him, you'll retreat from Him and others.**

In the moments of our deepest anguish and pain, I believe the Father wants nothing more than to comfort us and love us, in ways we would not experience had our pain not interrupted our plans. In some of my most agonizing moments, I can clearly see the invitation of the Father to silence the worries of this life and steal away with Him. I am comforted there by His deep, abiding love for me and I receive peace to endure or retreat from those things causing pain in my life.

When we are anxious we are often seeking an answer. Normally a yes or no, but if we quiet our spirits we can hear the Father's voice. Once, I was wanting an answer and I heard the words of my Father saying "you can't see it now daughter, but I am working." The answer did not give silence to my questions, but rather peace to my heart.

We long as humans for answers, but our Father longs for relationship. So although our questions motivate us to come to Him, He uses them to create relationship with us. The Bethel worship song Nearness speaks so clearly to this,

I stand with so many questions
But You know all of the answers
And whether this side of Heaven
I know that You are the Healer

And my heart will stay steadfast
I know that You are good
And my heart will stay steadfast
I know that You are good

Comforter You are to me

Shelter from the cold
Constant how You carry me
Never letting go
You are with me

Your voice holds me together
When I feel like I'm falling apart
I place my world in Your hands
You come and steady my heart

I feel you in the stillness
I know that You are good
I feel you in the stillness
I know that You are good

Our questions bring us to Him, and He creates that relationship with us where His voice can hold us together, our worries can dissipate and we can feel Him all around us-knowing that He is good. Look up and let Him heal you.

Your struggles give you a unique tool to reach others in love and freedom. If you haven't struggled, those who are won't want to listen to you. If you have a heart that understands, you will be able to minister to hearts in need. If you choose to take those moments of pain and seek out healing, you will indeed find it, and then be able to lead others to it as well.

Journal entry from April 11, 2018

"Today has been AMAZING! It's been such an awesome day and I've met so many awesome people and really enjoyed it. I've made connections with some awesome dudes and had such deep, meaningful and fun conversations. Yet even in the midst of laughter and pure joy, I heard the enemies' whispers..."You aren't being real. This is so fake!" And internally I stopped for a moment, then moved forward, the lie just grazing my soul, not completely gone but not being allowed to settle in.

What a master deceiver. What a creator of insecurity and division. What an absolute hater of my heart.

But the hate, it's merited, because I hate him too. I desire to see his kingdom fall as well, and it will. It has. My heart will settle in on the faithfulness of God before bed. Thank you Lord. Amen."

The Lord is so faithful to deliver us each step along the way. Often it doesn't feel good and there is a lot of pain involved but the Father has a purpose in it all. One of the greatest being, that you would **trust Him**. If you can take moments each day to remind yourself to look up, past all your circumstances and directly at the Father, He will work in your situation. **Change your focus. Set your gaze. Seal your purpose.**

The enemy's greatest goal is to steal. Without a proper perspective, he can steal our peace, our joy, and our purpose. Position your gaze. Not in, but up. **Choose to look at the Father, for He is looking at you!**

A Call to Courage!

"Be strong and courageous, all you who hope in the Lord!"
Psalm 31:24

Courage. It's that powerful tool that God requires of us to live lives that truly glorify Him. Courage. It's the ingredient needed to live successful, secure lives. Courage, it's what anxiety comes to drain every ounce of from you. Courage.

Every good story has a hero. A person who risks all to save the princess, or the city, or a dear friend who's been lost. And every great hero is just as human as you and me. But what sets the hero apart from the victim, is the courage they possess. Often times, they don't even realize what lies within them. What strong, bold power waits within to be unleashed. If only they would stop and ignite the great power concealed in them.

God calls His children to be courageous, yet sometimes courageous is the last thing the world, our friends, or we would even call ourselves. Exhausted by all we've endured, and lucky just to make it through the day. We don't want another challenge, we just want quiet, a couch, and Netflix. Stat. But God has called us to more! To adventure! To life! To courage! Steven Furtick said, in one of his messages, *"It takes faith to see your victory before you fight your battle."* That is the type of faith we must live with. One that is secure in our victory before we even begin the war.

It can almost seem intimidating until we remember we are not the ones navigating this ship or in charge of qualifying ourselves, He is! We do not produce the armor or fight the battle, He does. Our part is to use the armor and the Word He has given us to stand strong while our battle is being won.

2 Corinthians 3:4-6 says *"We are confident of all this because of our great trust in God through Christ. It is not that we think we are qualified to do anything on our own. Our qualification comes from God. He has enabled us to be ministers of his new covenant. This is a covenant not of written laws, but of the Spirit. The old written covenant ends in death; but under the new covenant, the Spirit gives life."* The word "qualified"

means officially recognized as being trained to perform a particular job.

Scripture tells us that we can't qualify or equip ourselves, He does that for us. So although I feel inadequate, insecure, and am easily timid, He has given me tools (Scripture, worship, and fellowship with Christ) that qualifies and strengthens me for the work at hand. Then when all is said and done, I have nothing to boast in but Christ alone (Galatians 6:14). I feel so inadequate in myself, but if I can get my eyes off me and onto Him, I can clearly see again. Once lost, I am quickly found by the One who loves me personally, and has qualified and called me, uniquely.

People need to see Jesus. Not us. They need to experience His love, not our broken counterfeits, and when we experience Him to that extent, that level, people will see Jesus in our eyes. In our expressions. They'll feel Him in our touch. We want people to experience Jesus, not us. Yet our brokenness is what highlights, to us and others, His power, strength, love and grace. It's what reveals to an insecure generation, a secure God.

I myself, would not know God's greatness had I not tasted my own defeats and inadequacies. I would not know He was greater than anything I would face, had I not faced some stuff. **Anxiety and fear came to steal from me, but God used them**

to strengthen me. Can you look back and see that in your story? In your depression. In your loneliness. In your anger. Can you see how God used it to make you into a caring person? A faithful friend. A tender mother. Acknowledge that in this moment.

The realization that what the enemy meant for evil, God will use for good, should awaken your courage as you trust in Him. He has you friend. His purpose will prevail, your part is to trust. We have to believe there is purpose in this. I have to. You have to. Otherwise, we'll be like lame hamsters on a wheel, just trying to get by. I don't want to get by. I want to make this count! I want a full life. A vigorous one. A makes me giddy and take the wind out of the enemy's sails kind of life.

That's the life we were meant to have.
That's the life we're going to get.
We have to have bold determination.

We have to look our fears square in the face and say *"I can't hear you."* We have to walk up to that insecurity and say- *"you don't know me."* We have to take hold of that addiction and say ***"you will not stop me from my purpose."*** Because at the end of the day that's what all these darts from the enemy are meant to do, stop us from our purpose.

The bigger that purpose, the bigger the battle. Your enemy can't have you living victorious and helping to set other captives free, that would derail his purpose-our destruction. Do you see friend, the enemy's purpose and ours are directly at war against each other. That's the battle. That's why we feel opposition, because it really does exist.

Think of the Jews for instance, God's holy people, yet throughout history the enemy has used every opportunity to destroy them from the face of the Earth. Why? Because they are chosen. You and I are chosen as well. We bear the mark, the image of our Creator. His plans and purposes are within our hearts, and to that end the devil's desire is to wipe us out. In a world where stress, pressure, fear and disappointment are around every corner, he takes advantage and uses this angle for his benefit. But we, can be wise to him and meet each challenge, and destructive obstacle with courage.

In my own life, the enemy has used abuse, small and large alike, to try to steal my destiny and derail my purpose. I went through two of the most trying years of my life when I had to remove from myself from an intimate relationship that was poisoning my growth and life.

My heart struggled. I cried a lot. I felt pain, guilt, and fear for the future all at the same time. I begged God to move, I went through all the stages of grief multiple times. Denial, anger, sadness…nothing changed, but I changed. In the darkest of times the Lord gave me something to hold onto. The first time I said it, it was as if God Himself had given me the words. I could not have thought of this on my own, especially since it wasn't a present reality.

It's for my kids.

"I'll go through anything I have to for my kids." Each time I said it, I cried. Such a deep, abiding love for my sweetest possessions, who do not yet exist. This strong statement gave me incredible courage for each obstacle I faced. I shook with righteous anger and the heat of boldness was felt in each tear. To this day, I would walk that painful journey all over again for those precious babies and the freedom they will one day live in.

What awakens your courage?

What creates a boldness and fire in you that cannot be put out by circumstance? Find that thing, lean into it, and allow God to use it. He wants to speak to it and use you there. That place could change your generation. That place could change generations after you. That place could shape the faith of many and create a lasting effect on those to come.

The Pleasure of Trusting God

"Unbelief is the mother of every anxiety."
John Calvin

trust/trest/"firm belief in the reliability, truth or strength of someone or something."
Synonyms: confidence, belief, faith, certainty, assurance, conviction, credence, reliable.[5]

Life is filled with so many ups and downs, so many uncertainties, so much joy and pain. What a gift to be able to trust the Giver of all life. How freeing to decide to see all of life as ordained,

---

[5] Trust. Accessed May 2015 through www.dictionary.com

watched over, and tended to by the Creator of the Universe.

How amazing to experience each day with the knowledge that the One who loves me and cares for me more than anyone, is with me and has given me the strength for each circumstance I will meet. My countenance goes from timid and fearful to empowered and bold, audacious and courageous!

My shoulders that once hung low are now held high, and a consistent smile graces my face. I begin to set aside fear and choose to embrace each new situation life brings. I resist all feelings of depression and discouragement because life is a gift and I've got too much to accomplish before He welcomes me home.

Isaiah 26:3 was a verse my mother taught me to cling to during times of uncertainty, but even more than clinging to, to boldly declare it as truth in my life. It says: *"You will keep in perfect peace those whose minds are steadfast, because they trust in You."*

The verses that precede and follow are just as powerful. They describe the righteous nation, those who have kept the faith, and the importance of trusting God forever!

Isaiah 26:1-4

In that day this song will be sung in the land of Judah: We have a strong city; God makes salvation its walls and ramparts. Open the gates that the righteous nation may enter, the nation that keeps faith. You will keep in perfect peace those whose minds are steadfast, because they trust in you.

Trust in the Lord forever, for the Lord, the Lord himself, is the Rock eternal.

Perfect peace. I want to live in that! I want my life to look like that! I want to be that! I want people to come in contact with me and say *"dang, something is different about her."* How does Scripture say we can receive that? By keeping our mind steadfast on the things of God (truth), and by trusting in Him. Do you act like you have assurance that God will move no matter how painful or tough the situation in your life may be?

Matthew Henry's Commentary says:

"All those minds shall be truly stayed, that are stayed on God. They shall be as Mount Zion, firm as it is; a mountain supported by providence much more as a hold mountain supported by promise. They cannot be removed from

confidence in God. They abide forever in that grace which is the earnest of their everlasting continuance in glory. Committing themselves to God, they shall be safe from their enemies. Even mountains may moulder and come to nothing, and rocks be removed, but God's covenant with His people cannot be broken, nor His care of them cease. Their troubles shall last no longer than their strength will bear them up under them."

Trust in God + Steadfast Mind= Perfect Peace

Complete dependence upon God and the things of God are key in thriving in a dark world where we are meant to shine as bright lights. The world needs to and wants to see our peace. Matthew Henry refers to this peace as "inward peace, outward peace, peace with God, peace with conscience, peace at all times and peace in all events."

What are the areas of your life that you find it hard to trust God? Take a few minutes and write them out and pray about those areas.

____

____

____

When we expose those areas to the Lord, ourselves, and others, they lose a grip on our hearts. Bringing light to darkness is the best way to begin your healing. Our hearts were meant to rest in Jesus and until that happens we will find ourselves striving and failing at life, all the while longing for the real answer to our freedom. Our freedom is found in the deepest places of His heart.

You are meaningful to the Kingdom! The enemy knows that, but do you?

Those of us who are attacked by anxiety, insecurity or fear, seem to be some of God's most sensitive children. Sensitive to His touch, but just as sensitive to the lies of the enemy and pervasive emotions. Our hearts' desire is to do what God created us to do, and to live the lives He desires of us. If we could keep the goal in mind: that which

God has called us to, we would be less easily distracted. We would set boundaries that help keep our souls secure and our hearts at peace, because we would be passionate and fixed on serving our purpose and leaving all else behind. We are children of the light-we can live lives that reflect that light.

If only we could recognize how valuable we are to the Kingdom, to the building up of other believers, and to the development of lost souls seeking Jesus. If only we could see what the enemy sees. We can. In part, by choosing to use the pain Satan has created in our lives for something eternal. That's why he attacked us in the first place is it not? To destroy our eternal purpose? Let's use our pain to counteract his purpose and fulfill God's eternal one, the saving of lost souls.

Let's let his contribution create a neon sign that points us to our destiny. Our places of deep hurt and longing create a pathway that the Lord can use to free others. What message has the enemy tried to convey to you in the darkest moments of your life? What cuts hurt so deeply that you hope no one ever knows about it?

The prescription to pain is PURPOSE! Within the pain lies our purpose, and to overcome the pain and live abundantly we need to be serving and fulfilling our purpose! I would prefer not to be the woman who tells the world she's had to deal with anxiety, but my pain has served a purpose. It will encourage other believers who are struggling, expose those seeking healing to the Healer, and revive my soul as I share. This is probably my favorite way to give the enemy a black eye!

Anxiety is so easily soothed when we get into His presence and understand who He really is. Every fear is quieted, each worry silenced. Only when we experience Him in those deep ways and through purposed prayer and fellowship with Him can our most broken places be healed.

One of the fastest ways to soothe anxiety and fear is to magnify the Father. That simply means to exalt Him above your circumstance and see Him for who He really is. The enemy was the first worshipper. His job was literally to praise and glorify God while leading all the angels in the worship of the Creator. One day, he became jealous of all the praise the Lord was getting and wanted it for himself. His desire lead him to create his own kingdom, one that is still at war with the purposes of God today. Sometimes, defeating his attacks is as easy as reminding him of who he was. A worshipper.

When we worship, we create an atmosphere where the enemy cannot penetrate our hearts, because they are fixed on the Savior. When we align our hearts and worship the Father, He comes and fights our battle. He inhabits the praises of His people (Psalm 22:3). Invite Him to fight for you. John 12:32 says *"And when I am lifted up from the earth, I will draw all people to myself."* His invitation stands. Create space to lift Him up and allow Him to draw you to His heart.

How can you experience deep peace in the midst of horrible and horrendous storms? **Focus**. The Bible tells us that *"As the mountains surround Jerusalem, so the Lord surrounds His people both now and forevermore"* (Psalm 125:2). When we gain the right perspective and understand that the God of the Universe (the One who created our innermost parts and knows us deeply) surrounds us, we can get a better grasp on life. He is for us. He loves us. He is with us.

We have to cling to those Scriptures that help us regain perspective. When you feel the ship swaying what can be the anchor that stabilizes you? Psalm 34:7 tells us that *"the angel of the Lord encamps round about them that fear Him, and He delivers them."* Angels are surrounding us! Let perspective sink in. Fight from that place.

"I have told you these things, so that in me you may have peace. In this world you will have trouble. But take heart! I have overcome the world."
John 16:33

When we spend time with Freedom (Jesus), we cannot help but live free. He gives us the capacity to hear and obey His Word (Psalm 40:6), and in doing so, we experience the depths of His love and freedom. The Word says that if we remain in Him, He will remain in us (John 15:4). When we can live from that place, we will live like never before!

The truth is the only thing that can change is the atmosphere! You must create an opportunity to bring truth to light. Call upon truth. Like the writer of Proverbs describes wisdom as supreme, and better than gold (Proverbs 4:7, Proverbs 16:16), truth is precious and it gives us the strength and boldness to live unfettered by life's demands and sudden changes. It is our anchor. What is truth? Truth embodied is Jesus, so if you need some help, let's look there.

God wants us so desperately to allow our pain to push us closer to Him, into a deeper, more meaningful relationship with the Father. Where we live as dearly loved children (Ephesians 5:1). His truth gives us the confidence to see, experience, and deal with our pain in healthy ways.

Psalm 16:5 says *"Lord, you alone are my portion and my cup; you make my lot secure."* He has us, we are secure in Him. Psalm 17:8 describes us as the apple of His eye. That means that we are the very center of His focus. We are *"hidden in the shadow of His wings"* (Psalm 91:4).

We have to restore our security and trust in God, and His infinite love for us. As our Father, He loves us deeply and passionately and seeks to protect us and provide for us. Psalm 27:5 says that *"in the day of trouble You will keep me safe."* God longs to come to our aid, we have to place our absolute trust and faith in Him. Without settling His Word and absolute security in our hearts we will be tempted to give into fear and insecurity, to doubt the incredible things God has in store for us and the plans of peace He has to comfort our hearts. **If we lose our focus, we forfeit our peace.**

Psalm 91:1 says *"He who dwells in the shelter of the Most High will rest in the shadow of the Almighty."* We have to learn to make Him our shelter. If we can create those times where we go to the shelter for protection, and ultimately make it a lifestyle of living in His shelter, we will be at rest. We will experience His infinite, deep, and undying love and peace.

I have a friend who is a major power house for Jesus. Girl can straight call down Heaven and preach the house down, but put her in one of these social settings and she breaks out in hives from her anxiety. The enemy thinks he'll cripple her with this insecurity, but he's so wrong. It takes on different forms in all of us, but the objective is the same. Little does he know though, that we have the power.

We have victory in Jesus. Read that again. It's true. It's real and available. The biggest hurdle is our belief. Belief that we are victorious. Belief that we are in Jesus. Belief that it will all be okay. When you feel out of control, victory is the last thing that comes to mind but it's yours, and it's mine.

Knowing the Father in a deep and abiding way changes everything. Knowing He already gave us victory, does as well. We can experience anything in this life without fear or shame. His Word tells us that perfect love casts out all fear (1 John 4:18). When we know His perfect love, we are not afraid. We aren't afraid to make mistakes, to talk to Daddy about our sin, to experience pain…because we know He loves us, is with us, and for us. When you get a vision of how much he loves you, personally, you understand that you can fight any demon, deal with any lie, and challenge any secret sin because He is with you.

God's love is the most incredible and special gift He has given us. If I know He really loves me, I'm not afraid of people's opinion of me, or my own. If I know He really loves me… I'm a child of peace. I know that though man throw the dice, God determines the outcome (Proverbs 16:33). I can trust Him to be God in my life and rule and reign in every area. My job is to give Him control and to stop fighting for it. To release my life and it's ultimate outcome to His capable hands. What an incredible level of peace this creates as my trust goes deep.

My life doesn't belong to me. My family doesn't belong to me. My job doesn't define me. My income is not my security. That's so freeing! It is so empowering if I can really understand and accept that from my loving Father. I have no "cares" in this life because **everything belongs to Him and He will provide for any need I have.** The world is a scary place when we don't have an all-knowing Father protecting us and tending to our most minute needs. Panic arises from misplaced trust.

Really stop and think. This isn't meant to create more panic, but really what in this life do we have control of? Everything is subject to change based on the direction of the Father. Everything. So how much more wise would we be to trust and not be afraid?

We can be so easily distracted by all the cares and concerns of this life, that we take our eyes off of Jesus, and like Peter, begin to sink. I've felt that sinking feeling when I've lost sight of Jesus. My stomach sinks. My heart sinks. My spirit sinks. It's all about perspective. It has to be fixed on Jesus! It is so easy to stay focused on life's demands, our pursuits, and the pressures of everyday and lose sight of Jesus. **But if we want to stand and not sink we have to fix our eyes on Him!**

I find it incredibly difficult sometimes to really trust God. I mean really allowing Him to have control of every area of my life. It's painful and scary, and sometimes, I honestly don't know how! Often I'm so consumed with my own panic and in problem solving mode that I can't unclench my fingers and trust Him, and it only hurts me. If I could let go I'd see His hand there all along. And I'd be able to **give into grace.** I would accept His gift and deny the lie that He doesn't love me or have good things in store for me.

This life will drag us in so many directions, but if we can secure our anchor in Jesus, we will have the staying power that keeps us from crashing on the rocks. Our faith does not make us immune to pain in this life, but gives us power to be more than overcomers. Let's live victorious. Let's sink our teeth into the gospel and live changed.

In Scripture, it talks about literally eating the scroll (Ezekiel 3:3). This is about taking the Word of God and allowing it into the deepest places. Your perspective will change if you digest the Word into your spirit. Let's shape our perspective with truth and love given to us directly from our Heavenly Father. The world becomes a better place when we understand, accept, and see things through the Father's eyes.

When we acknowledge pain, discover truth, and experience life through the lense of the One who created each moment, each trial, each blessing, to shape us into the person we are to be, then and only then will we be able to fully trust in and rely on Him. Knowing He has what is best for us in His timing.

If I am able to see each setback, each set up, each failure, each promotion as a gift from God, I will then be able to recognize and accept each moment as a gift from Him. Seeing His hand in it all. His purpose. His ultimate progression for my life.

As people, we often find it so hard to trust. To be honest, it can be hard to trust others who willingly or unknowingly hurt us. So, it can be extremely difficult to trust an unseen God. One we don't truly believe has our best interest at heart, one that we don't truly understand, and one we don't believe fully understands us. How can we trust Him?

Throughout my own life I've found it extremely difficult because not only do I not trust others, and question if I can trust God... but I don't trust me. I wonder if I'll make a mistake, if I'm doing something wrong, or if I'm missing the ultimate purpose for which I'm on this earth. I get caught up in my own pursuit for peace, and in doing so miss my purpose. I wander around looking for significance and all the while miss small and big opportunities God has placed all around me.

So many trials and emotions are a direct result of our lack of trust in our Heavenly Father. I'm sitting here now in absolute awe of God and all the trust He so deserves from me. I remember one night my heart was so heavy that when I woke up I was in dire need of God for the day. I could see He was orchestrating things, but it didn't make the process any easier. I continued to worry about details, both big and small, and decisions that I believed "rested on my shoulders." How wrong I was. When I decided to stop the merry-go-round, and focus on others, asking how I could pray for close friends and family, God intervened in my life and answered a desperate prayer of my heart. Through focusing on the needs of others in prayer, God answered mine and set me free. He brought peace in the midst of pain. How could I not trust

Him? Why was I so unwillingly believing He would not only answer the cries of my heart, but be intricately involved?

He wants more than anything else for us to truly trust Him. With everything. With all we are and all we have. If we can truly trust Him, then we can trust His <u>entire</u> Word and experience peace and purpose! Think about that. Our lack of trust and lack of knowledge in God's' Word reveals we don't believe His Word to be the Truth. If we did, even when all hell is breaking loose in our lives, we could stand on scripture and know lasting peace. Just the thought of it makes me excited, calm and sensitive to a potential interaction with Daddy. The Word has that power. Let it meet you in your brokenness as you learn to trust Him more.

Spiritual Authority is the Cure

The enemies' number one goal is to keep us from understanding who we truly are so that he can deceive and destroy us. Let me say that again: he wants to kill you, and unless you know who you are, whose you are, and what rightfully belongs to you, he will succeed.

"But blessed is the man who trusts in the Lord, whose confidence is in Him."
Jeremiah 17:7

Ironically enough, right now I am under attack. The enemy has subtly gotten in my head this week without my complete knowledge and now I awaken to hives and an underlying surge of painful emotions. Through dreams sending subtle messages into my heart, photos of my abuser on Facebook, and conversations I have been a part of full of reminders of shame and guilt. I have been given the opportunity to forget who I am and the authority I have in Jesus.

Soldiers know they have to always be ready for battle. They keep their gear close and are available at a moment's notice. When we're told that we are in a battle, why do we not realize the importance of the same tactics? I mean He promised us troubles but told us to take heart. Therefore, we should anchor our hearts in Him and prepare our minds for the daily battles that lie ahead. The Bible literally describes the armor that the Lord has created for and given to us. We are in a battle.

Look at God's promise in scripture; Jeremiah 1:5, *"No one will be able to stand against you, as long as you live. For I will be with you as I was with Moses. I will not fail you or abandon you."* Thank you Jesus for truth in the middle of the storm. You are greater than anything I face; any lie, any pain, any problem. Jesus died for us to experience ultimate freedom and with His completed work on the cross, it is finished! Authority is ours. It was bought with His blood! Now, we can boldly walk in it. We have access to the authority that is available through the finished work of Christ!

The enemy's plan to destroy us is all in the hopes of keeping God's kids quiet. Throughout the last few days of nightmares, I've felt myself withdrawing, losing some of my new found boldness in God and confidence in who He created me to be! Ahhhaaa!! Wait? Do you see that? Slowly a little fox has trampsed his way into my vineyard. Now, it is my job to identify him, grab him by his little throat and throw him out of my beautiful garden! Forever! Gone! Back to boldness and confidence, and Christ centered freedom. That is the authority Christ died to give me at work in my life.

"I'm falling prey to the anxieties of my life once again. The demands, the desires, the issues, the pain…all of it washing over me and causing a storm of incredible proportions. Once again I'm caught looking inside myself trying to figure out what is wrong with me? Why can't I master this stuff? Why am I so overwhelmed? I'm left feeling like I can't do this and I should give up."

Journal entry from May 12, 2015

Wow. Can you say tactical strategy? The enemy of our souls watches us so closely. He knows our weaknesses, he knows our pain, and he knows that button that knocks you off the horse each time you try to ride off into the sunset. We've got to get serious about fighting back, about holding onto our authority and boldly using it to destroy strongholds.

It is not an easy task and this battle is for the strong at heart. As we continue though, to grow in our knowledge of who we are, the fight becomes easier, and the battles shorter. Recognizing the enemy and his tactics become easier to decipher and quicker to destroy.

As we discover God's truth it becomes easier to identify counterfeits. The lies that come in, like little foxes, because we all know that with each lie the enemy tells us, there is some small part of truth associated with it. That's how he deceives us. He takes a small truth and creates a giant lie. It's disguised of course. Yet, as we grow in our knowledge of God's truth we can quickly shoot down lies before they get the best of us.

These thinly disguised lies are meant to shoot our hearts into deep mistrust and ultimately broken fellowship with the Father. So as to outwit the nitwit, we must **seek first God's kingdom and His righteousness! His way of being made right** (Matthew 6:33). As we discover more about God's character, He reveals to us more about ours, and we can then shake off the lies with authority and power! Without knowing the Creator, it is hard to understand His creation, us. When we take time to delve into His heart, we better understand what our hearts are meant to be and do. We are broken vessels, but we display His glory and we have the ability in Christ to overcome this world and all that our enemy throws at us. It begins with our perspective of who we are in Christ.

My mentor, as a child, was taught by her father that when she walked into a place where she felt uncomfortable or even a little afraid, to straighten up and if anyone talked to her to confidently say "my father owns this place." She said it made such a difference in her overall demeanor and was a game changer. How cool that we can do that in life- because it's true! How awesome **to know, understand, and live like our Dad owns the place and has it all under control?! Because He does!** If we could meet life with that confidence, we would live well!

We would live assured that He hears us. At peace with our pasts and excited about our bright futures. Free from the heavy yokes of baggage we've been carrying around. I know that it's easy to read things on a page or hear it in a message, but it's a whole other thing to experience it in your life. I know all so well. But the Father desires for you, me, and every one of His children to experience this depth of security, love, and peace. To live in it daily we have to be willing to grow and create opportunities to hear from Him. To be assured of His deep, abiding, **surrounding** love.

I spent a weekend away with the Father and that was the Word He spoke to me. I read a passage and it came off the page. Surround. His Word says that as the mountains surround Jerusalem, so God surrounds His people (Psalm 125:2). As an Israel lover, I was able to vividly picture the mountains surrounding Jerusalem, and grasp the way God surrounds us. To understand that He surrounds us, creates a new level of security and peace in our souls. We can rest if we know He surrounds us, supports us and shields us.

We have to aggressively seek that greatness that God has planted within us. It serves a purpose not only for us, but for other special kingdom kids. God has given us the opportunity to live as a giant billboard pointing others to Jesus. Fear cannot hold us back!

Throughout scripture God used people who were terrified of their destiny. They not only couldn't recognize it, but it literally scared the bejesus out of them! Think of Joseph. This guy had challenge after challenge, and even with dreams of what lie ahead, he must have felt confusion or fear as he waited in a prison for his purpose to take form.

That gives me peace to know that I am not alone. If the saints in the faith struggled with this and still gained victory I am confident I can as well. Stand up sister! Stand up brother! Stand up child of God and boldly live with God's absolute truth settled in your heart. You are chosen, you are loved, you have been liberated by the King. Seek truth and say goodbye to lies!

You must daily make the choice to be prepared for battle. When we begin to win areas in our lives the enemy will try his hardest to subtly shift into another area. Disguising himself in a new arena of your life. Watch out for false accusations. Dreams, negative words from others, perverted thoughts... When he can't derail you, he can get _you_ to deny your destiny. It is equally important that you win areas in your life as you "scout out" and safeguard others. Know whose you are and then live in that confidence.

The process to healing looks different for everyone. No equation can be used to mathematically quantify pain and how you heal from it. It's a journey that serves an ultimate purpose, our healing and a deeper intimacy with our Creator we would never have known without the struggle. With this journey comes ups and downs. Sometimes these ups are crazy high and then we hit a low that sinks our ship and we lose hope.

Let me save me you some shame friends. I do not believe that we should use substances to dull our pain (most of my closest friends will tell you, I'm all about encouraging you to see the root and work to find healing in that place with God through journaling, deep questions, counseling, friends who keep you accountable, etc), but there are times, dear ones, when medication is needed.

I was one who fought it for many reasons...maybe pride, appearance, fear. Maybe all of those. But during a very difficult time in my life a counselor told me, it's a season, you do not have to choose this forever, but in this season it will be something that helps better equip you to deal with these challenges.

The Lord knows your heart friend. I am not encouraging you to use medication as a crutch, but rather to recognize that although our churches often frown on it, at times it is needed when you are sick. Sick of heart, sick of life, sick of love. I want shame to be stripped from you. There is no shame in the freedom God wants you to taste!

I say that in the midst of so many stories of people choosing death over a prescription. See momentary humiliation, as a cure. Friend, your story will be so great once you have walked this road with Jesus. Venture on. Use the tools you've been given and release any guilt or shame you may feel.

Remember that ultimately this journey of healing is meant to bring you to Jesus. Whether you use all the tools you're given, or just what you need to survive is up to you. Just get to Jesus, friend. He's waiting. He's so willing and ready to heal you. He knows the pain you are carrying and He wants to wipe away every tear. Scripture tells us that He literally keeps track of all our tears (Psalm 56:8). That's how much He loves you. Don't let shame hide you from His face.

Let's Get Practical...
Here to There

Each story is different. Each journey weaves down a different path, but we all have the same purpose: to be image bearers of the King. If that is our truth, then we can live in the joy of knowing He will indeed set us free and set us on a path to purpose. There will be valleys and there will be mountains. Both will come and both will forever change us.

So, how do we move forward and live in freedom from our fears and pain? We lay ourselves at the feet of Jesus. Without serious and intentional moments with the Father, we are immune to the healing power available to us. **God desires to set us free more than we desire to be free.** We have to believe that and live like it. Courageous, bold, unashamed of our wounds, they will be what sets others free. It's the power of our testimony.

Our generation is probably the most authentic to ever walk this planet. We don't want to hide behind labels, denominations, political parties or organizations. We want to be people, who engage people. What an awesome group for God to use. What a serious target to the enemy. We have power in our hands, our testimony. So there is no doubt that he wants to keep us from experiencing healing because then we would not turn back and set others free.

Healing for me, and for most, takes time. We wake up one day and realize, He did it. We just faithfully sowed seeds and believed Him for it and it happened! Be faithful where you are, friends. That's where God has you and wants you to thrive. His purpose for you there, is good. Just think, maybe your healing resides in that house. **Be sure to be plugged into a local church body.**

Next, serve. Serving causes me to focus on others and their needs, and keeps my eyes off me. When insecurity strikes, it is easy to turn inward, when we were meant to live in relationship. It's a catch 22. We feel the pain of the lack of relationship, but we can't figure out our stuff and how to thrive, so we shrink back. Get out and serve! Being with others who have a similar heart and loving others in need, changes your heart and is a wonderful reality check. Serve.

So often when I'm anxious, the fastest way to get back into alignment with peace is through **worship**. Think about that. Not only does it refocus our hearts back on Christ, but it uses the enemy's natural gifting of glorifying God. He was the head worshipper. When my heart is at war within me, worship can lead me right back into freedom. Singing, dancing, humming worship... try it friend. Find freedom in the darkest places, He's there. The psalmist said anywhere he went, God was there (Psalm 139:8) if I even go to the depths of hell, you are there. No matter what you are facing He is there. In your midst. Call out to Him.

When the wheels of fear and anxiety are turning, our insides tense up. **Get out!** Go for a walk, meet a friend for dinner, go see a movie, or take a budgeted shopping trip. Do something that literally stops the cycle in your head. If you can't get the thoughts to stop enough to be able to leave, journal them out and then walk away.

Journaling is so important for processing and for deep healing. Can't think of what to journal? Go deep. What am I feeling? When did it start? Why? What am I believing? What's truth? Get to the heart of the matter and reveal what is actually happening. Once you have, walk away and go do something else. I am a HUGE proponent of journaling! Like for real though... it's awesome! I have watched friends struggle and strain through a situation and then challenged them to get alone with their journal and Jesus and write out what is on their heart and mind, and almost instantly their perspective shifts. They do not experience absolute peace until they allow the Father to enter into their situation, but the act of writing out the issue at heart brings clarity to their current state of mind. When emotions come in and cloud our judgement it can be hard to see what the real issue at hand is. Taking time to journal can help clarify the situation.

During dark times, we often isolate ourselves, when we were created for relationship and need it to thrive. Choose to **be social** even when you don't feel like it. Your feelings will eventually line up with what your heart truly needs during this time. You may feel awkward, like everyone can see how you feel on the inside, but they can't. Others are in their own form of pain. We need each other. In my circle, we call this our village. These women ferociously love one another. We will drop everything to be there for one of our village members. This village is made up of like minded people who are full of love, grace, wisdom and determination. **Create a village**. Surround yourself with people who will do this journey with you and will help you to do it well. When panic arises and you feel alone or are thinking too much, call for your village.

Someone who should be an extension of your village is an amazing counselor. Don't wait until you are at the end of your rope to understand that your mental health is just as important as your physical health. We are so uniquely made and engage others on all levels; emotionally, mentally, physically, spiritually. Make sure you are in-tune to each part of your makeup. Make your soul a priority. **Find a counselor** you can connect with. Finding a good counselor is difficult, so be patient and try out a few until you find one that fits you. This awesome relationship exists. I have one!

The greatest way to live in freedom, is to invite others into your journey. To refine you, correct you, and help point you to truth when your world has spun out of control.

Another way that I personally redirect my energy is in what I call "**geeking out**." For me personally that looks like choosing something to study in Scripture. A theme, a word, a number...and then once I've chosen it, I hone in and learn all I can about it. Maybe you like photography, and can use this time to download videos on techniques or read a book on implementing better strategies to your systems. Whatever it may be, go at it hard! Pour all your energy into that thing and use it as an opportunity for growth not restriction.

Focus on the light. This is a practice that is both physical and spiritual in application. A friend of mine was hospitalized for chest pain, and when the panic attacks were heightened, a doctor had her stare into the light bulb above her. The panic attacks would immediately subside because there is something about light that causes our brains to regroup. Think about how natural light helps you wake up in the morning. There is something special about light, and the light of the Father definitely takes the cake!

As humans we have this deep longing to be accepted, and in that deep longing, we often are sensitive to and push away correction. Sadly in doing so we miss a crucial component of our salvation and the opportunity to experience personal growth in highlighted areas. The Bible teaches that God corrects, based on His love for us.

Throughout life you will have many opportunities to become bitter and resort to pain, when life is trying to teach us and God is giving us an opportunity for growth. This is probably the most challenging area, but being teachable can make our life better overall and keep us living in consistent peace. **Be teachable.**

Another awesome tool that helps in times of anxiety and is probably one of my favorite ways to slap the enemy when he's trying to kick me and get me down, is to text ten people and ask how can I **pray** for them. Take your focus off of you and put it on your Father and His power and heart to heal, restore, set free and bring peace to others. In that you are freed. He has the same heart for you.

His divine power has given us everything we need for a godly life through our knowledge of him who called us by his own glory and goodness.
2 Peter 1:3

This life is meant to be lived well. Take each tool you've been given to succeed and use it. Watch as the Father uses each trial and each bump in the road to create a greater depth in you and in this generation. We have been marked for a reason and a purpose. Let's pursue it. Let's live boldly and without apology. Let's make a mark on our world for our Savior and never let it be the same!

I love you dear one!
Light the torch and pass it on!

Holly Hungerford

LET US NOT

BECOME

WEARY

IN DOING

GOOD, FOR

AT THE

PROPER

TIME WE

WILL REAP

A HARVEST

IF WE DO

NOT GIVE

UP.

GALATIANS 6:9

Join the Journey

The Set Apart One blog is a community of individuals journeying together with God. By connecting with us, you'll engage in conversation with the Set Apart One team and community to gain accountability, acceptance, and love. Our hope is that through Set Apart One, you'll be able to foster friendships that are vulnerable and life-giving.

Through this blog, you'll get fresh encouragement and a relevant word from the blog team. Our goal is to provide the tools you need to remain faithful to your walk with God. You'll read pieces from others who are unafraid to take off the masks and get real with those they encounter. Each post will challenge and ignite the flame within you to continue in pursuit of deep, authentic, and vulnerable conversations and relationships.

Our hope is that your love for Jesus will grow deeper and greater so that you can continue to love others well. We want to be a resource to you as you journey through relationship with God and others, because we truly believe that you have been set apart for something special and unique for the glory of our Heavenly father.

Setapartone.com

Questions for the author?
holly@setapartone.com

Holly Hungerford is a daughter, sister, and a friend to many. She is a writer and entrepreneur of people. Holly loves to grow relationships and build others up into the people God has created them to be so they can live to their full potential in Christ. She is a graduate of Southeastern University with a degree in Church Ministries and over a decade of experience serving in the local church. Her intense testimony includes being delivered from deep emotional wounds and traumatic symptoms she incurred from relational abuse. She lives to reveal the power that can come from bringing those wounds to the Father to be healed and learning how to live from a place of freedom. Holly desires to serve you as a sister and friend as you seek the true freedom that comes from your Father who intimately loves you and has good things in store for you.

Made in the USA
Columbia, SC
06 November 2019